BATTLE
IN THE
MIND

by
Bill Basansky

Harrison House
Tulsa, Oklahoma

Battle in the Mind
ISBN 0-89274-022-1
Copyright © 1976 by Bill Basansky
P. O. Box 7126
Fort Myers, Florida 33911

Published by Harrison House, Inc.
P.O. Box 35035
Tulsa, Oklahoma 74153

Contents

To contact the author,
write:
Bill Basansky
Love and Grace Fellowship
P. O. Box 7126
Fort Myers, Florida 33911

*Please include your prayer requests
and comments when you write.*

1

The Fruitful Christian Life

For though we walk in the flesh, we do not war after the flesh:

(For the weapons of our warfare are not carnal, but mighty through God to the pulling down of strong holds;)

Casting down imaginations, and every high thing that exalteth itself against the knowledge of God, and bringing into capitivity every thought to the obedience of Christ.

2 Corinthians 10:3-5

In this scripture we definitely see two distinct and opposite battles that are constantly going on in the mind of every Christian. The Spirit wrestles against the flesh and the flesh against the Spirit. Here, in order to be victorious, God requires of you to confess His Word regardless of your feelings; yield to the Spirit of God, who is the lover of your soul, and resist the temptation of your flesh, and then the devil will flee from you (James 4:7-8).

In this battle between the flesh and the spirit it is important to know what God expects of us. But it is equally as important to know what God does not expect of us. Philippians 2:12 says,

Work out your own salvation with fear and trembling.

This then, speaks of something we have to do. But the next verse says,

For it is God which worketh in you both to will and to do of his good pleasure.

That says what we are not able to do, God will do.

Christian growth is a cooperative work between believer and God which produces a ripe and fruitful Christian life. Trying to do what is not our part, or what is not promised for us by God, is as great a mistake as neglecting to do what *is* our part. Indeed, one of the enemy's cleverest tools is to entice many believers into doing that which is not expected of them — and thereby discouraging them so that they end up not even doing that which is expected and possible.

What is our part and what is God's part in this cooperative undertaking?

Two passages of Scripture will provide clarification on this subject.

> **Behold, thou desirest truth in the inward parts: and in the hidden part thou shalt make me to know wisdom.** (The Psalmist is saying: please teach me wisdom in my inward being and in my secret heart.)
>
> **Purge me with hyssop, and I shall be clean: wash me, and I shall be whiter than snow.**
>
> **Make me to hear joy and gladness.**
>
> **Create in me a clean heart, O God; and renew a right spirit within me.**
>
> **Cast me not away from thy presence; and take not thy holy spirit from me.**
>
> **Restore to me the joy of thy salvation; and uphold me with thy free** (willing) **spirit.**
>
> **Psalm 51:6-8a, 10-12**

In these verses you can see who is acted upon by whom, and who it is that brings truth in the inward part of the heart of man. It is God who teaches, washes us with His blood, purges, restores, fills, creates and upholds us with His hand of righteousness.

Whatever change takes place deep within an individual's heart is the work of God.

In Colossians 3:10-16 (RSV) we read:

> **And have put on a new nature, which is being renewed in knowledge after the image of its**

6

creator...put on then, as God's chosen ones, holy and beloved, compassion, kindness, lowliness, meekness and patience, forebearing one another and, if one has a complaint against another, forgive each other; as the Lord has forgiven you, so you also must forgive. And above all these, put on love, which binds together in perfect harmony...let the peace of Christ rule in your hearts...and the Word of Christ dwell in you richly....

It is obvious in these verses that God's chosen people, the believers, must change their attitudes, discipline themselves in their minds and will, to put on love, compassion, kindness, meekness, etc. The outward visible work of "putting on" is the work of the believer and all of this is done in the mind, by being willing to think like God (Phil. 4:8). While the believer puts on the outward form of Christ, God being the Potter works the inner change of the heart of man.

In Galatians 5:16 (RSV) Paul says: **...do not fulfill the lust** (desires) **of the flesh.** Paul does not say, do not *have* the desires, but he is saying do not *fulfill* (gratify) them. In other words, Paul is telling the believer do not allow them outward expression.

Our old nature stirs up a desire in the soul to strike back and hurt those who have done us wrong. Our soulish part only loves when it's being loved and wants to strike back when it's being hurt.

An example of soulish love is found in the well-known song: "Frankie (who loved her man) shot him because he done her wrong." But God's kind of love loves even when the one you love hurts you.

A further example of God's love is when Jesus said:

Father, forgive them; for they know not what they do.

Luke 23:34

Now Galatians 5:16 does not indicate that you shouldn't *feel* that way. It simply states: "Don't fulfill the lust of the flesh." (Don't carry out your fleshly cravings,

7

do not gratify the desires of the flesh.) Do not let gossip come out of your mouth. Do not say anything that will cause another person to be hurt. That which is still-born is not alive and cannot grow (Prov. 18:21; Matt. 12:34).

As you build this outward form of self-control, in faith that God will fill it, God takes the responsibility of replacing that desire of the flesh with the fruits of the Spirit.

> ...**but though our outward man perish** (the desires of the flesh diminish), **yet the inward man is renewed day by day.**
>
> 2 Corinthians 4:16

Sanctification is truly the work of grace. Yet we have had a part in it. Our God gives faith (Rom. 12:3) and has constructed a vessel which could receive His gracious work, for God does not pour out His grace where there is no faith to receive it.

This then is the mystery of sanctification. We need to construct the outward vessels of holiness with expectant faith; that God will fill them, and Christ Jesus the hope of glory will enter in and set up His kingdom within you (Luke 17:21), which is not meat or drink but righteousness, right relationships and standing with God. It is peace, perfect peace within us, that passes all understanding with the natural mind, and joy — joy unspeakable and full of glory, the Shekinah glory of God, which will radiate through your being.

> **Faithful is he that calleth you, who also will do it.**
>
> 1 Thessalonians 5:24

In John 12:24 Jesus said:

> **Verily, verily, I say unto you, Except a corn of wheat fall into the ground and die, it abideth alone: but if it die, it bringeth forth much fruit.**

The secret of a fruitful Christian life is not in *doing* but in *dying* — dying to self (fleshly desires), so that the indwelling life of Christ can be released, and in making Christian living not a duty but an exciting adventure with Christ.

2

Battle in the Mind

It says in 2 Corinthians 5:17,

> ...if any man be in Christ, he is a new creature: old things are passed away; behold, all things are become new.

That means that all things, those which were done in your life before, are no longer in your life. They are forgotten.

In Galatians 2:20 Paul is speaking and says, **"I am crucified with Christ: nevertheless I live...."** Old things are passed away, behold all things have become new. The old things that we have done before are gone, washed away with the blood of Christ and Paul says, **I am crucified with Christ: nevertheless I live; yet not I, but Christ liveth in me.** He says this temple (body) of mine is for the Holy Spirit. I don't do the things I used to do. He says, "I am crucified with Christ."

When you are *crucified*, you are dead. *You are dead to the old things.* You are dead to the *old man*, to the *old flesh*, and now, you *live for Jesus.*

Many Christians say that they are crucified with Christ, but in reality they have only fainted.

That's the problem with most Christians. They are not dead to old things, they have only fainted, and they rise up and do their own thing whenever they feel like it.

But Paul said, "I am crucified with Christ: nevertheless I live; yet not I, but *Christ liveth in me.*"

Now, if Christ lives in you, governs you, directs you, and guides you, you no longer will do or think the things that you've done in the past, but you will do and think the things that this new life in Christ Jesus is telling you to do.

Continuing with verse 20, Paul is saying,

> ... **nevertheless I live; yet not I, but Christ liveth in me: and the life which I now live in the flesh I live by the faith of the Son of God, who loved me, and gave himself for me.**

He is saying to you and me that his life is completely different now, and he has turned the opposite direction, because the old man is dead, and he is a brand new creature in Christ.

As a Christian, a person must realize that his life is changed and that he must "live by the faith of the Son of God."

Second Corinthians 5:17 reads: ...**if any man be in Christ, he is a new creature.**

My Russian Bible reads a little differently. It states, "...*if any human being* (that includes man, woman, boy or girl) *be in Christ, he is a new creature.*" He is a new individual. He has a new personality, and this new personality is no longer like Bill Basansky used to be, but it's now after the personality and likeness of our Lord Jesus Christ.

Philippians 2:5 reads:

> **Let this mind be in you, which was also in Christ Jesus.**

Paul says, "the old things that I've done no longer interest me. I am now searching for the new things because a new person dwells in me and desires the things of God. My mind has become one with God.

3
The Temple of God

The new man is now thinking about the things of God and not the things of the world.

What can be done about the carnal mind? What can be done about the desires of the flesh?

Paul writes in Romans 12:1 and tells us,

> I beseech you therefore, brethren, by the mercies of God, that ye present your bodies a living sacrifice, holy, acceptable unto God, which is your reasonable service.

Paul said, "...present your bodies...present your temples, holy and acceptable unto God." God does not require anything of us that is unreasonable!

You must do the presenting of yourself, just as you are, to God, and then He will do the accepting and the cleansing.

First Corinthians 3:16,17 states:

> Know ye not that ye are the temple of God, and that the Spirit of God dwelleth in you?
>
> If any man defile the temple of God, him shall God destroy; for the temple of God is holy, which temple ye are.

The Bible reads in Matthew 6:24 that you can't serve two masters, for either you will hate the one, and love the other; or else you will hold to the one, and despise the other. You cannot serve God and the devil and expect God to protect you. You must choose who you are going to serve. The choosing is entirely up to you. This involves your mind and will, which is the soulish part of a human being.

God doesn't choose whom you should serve; you must make that choice yourself, even as Joshua did when he said:

> ...choose this day whom you will serve, but as for me and my house, we will serve the Lord.
>
> Joshua 24:25 RSV

He says in His Word that if you are doing something that gives glory to the devil, and is harmful to the body, and you like it, that the thing unleashed in your body is a joining of yourself to the world.

> What? know ye not that he which is joined to an harlot is one body? for two, saith he, shall be one flesh.
>
> 1 Corinthians 6:16

> A double minded man is unstable in all his ways.
>
> James 1:8

Double minded people on one hand want the blessings of God, and on the other hand they will go around the corner and get things from the devil.

You can't fellowship with the devil and with God at the same time.

In 1 Corinthians 6:17 Paul says,

> But he that is joined unto the Lord is one spirit.

Well, praise God! If you are a Christian joined to the Lord, then you are one spirit with God.

The Bible says in Isaiah 55:6-9,

> Seek ye the Lord while he may be found, call ye upon him while he is near:
>
> Let the wicked forsake his way, and the unrighteous man his thoughts: and let him return unto the Lord, and he will have mercy upon him; and to our God, for he will *abundantly pardon*.
>
> For my thoughts are not your thoughts, neither are your ways my ways, saith the Lord.
>
> For as the heavens are higher than the earth, so are my ways higher than your ways, and my thoughts than your thoughts.

He said it clearly, ''For my thoughts are not your thoughts, neither are my ways your ways....''

He says when you are joined unto the Lord as one spirit, *my ways are your ways and your ways are my ways.*

12

I and my Father are one.

John 10:30

That's the way it should be between a son and a father. When a son and a father have no relationship they have no communication between them. They then go their different ways.

The Bible teaches us in 1 Corinthians 6:18,19:

Flee fornication. Every sin that man doeth is without the body; but he that committeth fornication sinneth against his own body.

What? know ye not that your body is the temple of the Holy Ghost which is in you...?

Your body has been made for the Holy Ghost to dwell in, but you have to choose in your mind whom you will serve. God or the devil?

Some may ask, "How do I know when the enemy speaks to me?"

You will know when the enemy speaks to you to do something "under-handed." He speaks to you in your ear and tempts you to do wrong. When you have given your temple to God, you will refrain from doing wrong. When you trust Jesus, you follow Him completely. You live with the real person...JESUS. You serve Him and Him only.

Jesus said,

My sheep hear my voice, and I know them, and they follow me.

John 10:27

A person may say, "How do I know which of my thoughts are of God?"

You should *ask* God. *God wants you to talk to him.* If you want to know the truth, He'll show you, because He lives in you.

As we pointed out previously, Paul, in writing to the church at Corinth, asked, "What? know ye not that your body is the temple of the Holy Ghost which is in you?'' And Jesus said in John 16:14,

>He shall glorify me: for he shall receive of mine, and *shall shew it unto you.*

If your body (the temple) belongs to God, then your mind also belongs to God.

Paul relates this in Romans 12:1,

>I beseech you therefore, brethren, by the mercies of God, that ye present your bodies (He didn't say your spirits. He said, ye present your bodies unto Him) a living sacrifice, holy, acceptable unto God, which is your reasonable service.

God will not ask anyone to do anything that is unreasonable.

4

Be Ye Transformed

While living on the earth, Jesus was tempted of the devil. Because He was tempted, He is able to say to us that there is a way of escape. First Corinthians 10:13 (RSV) states:

> **No temptation has overtaken you that is not** *common* **to man. God is faithful, and he will not let you be tempted beyond your strength, but with the temptation will also provide the way to** *escape,* **that you may be able to endure it.**

You don't have to worry about escaping from the devil. He'll run from you when your mind is submitted to God and you are renewed and filled with His Word.

> **Submit yourselves therefore to God. Resist the devil, and he will flee from you.**
>
> **James 4:7**

Paul writes in Romans 12:2,

> **And be not conformed to this world: but be ye transformed by the renewing of your mind....**

The words *conformed* and *world* should be noted. Paul is warning the Christians not to act like the man of the world does, because the devil is the god of this world. That is why we are not to think and reason as a man of this world thinks and reasons, for though we live in the world we are not of this world. That is why he indicates that we should be *transformed* by the renewing of our minds.

Transforming means "changing". Whatever you were before becomes changed. You are the one who has the authority over your mind. This is a gift of God for every human being...the wonderful "right" to choose what a person shall be.

Romans 12:2 continues: ...be ye *transformed* by the *renewing of your mind,* that ye may prove what is that good, and acceptable, and perfect will of God.

The Amplified Bible reads in the same scripture,

Do not be conformed to this world — this *age,* fashioned after and adapted to its external, superficial customs. But be transformed (changed) by the [entire] renewal of your mind — by its new ideals and its new attitude — so that you may prove [for yourselves] what is the good and acceptable and perfect will of God, even the thing which is good and acceptable and perfect [in His sight for you].

The Bible speaks about the mind of man. It says, ...be not *conformed to this world* but be *transformed.* The word *conformed* means don't be "fashioned" or "molded," or, don't be "like the world." Don't be the sheep and don't be the follower of the whims of the world. Don't pride yourself in being conventional, because that which we call *conventional* is just being fashioned as to the things of this world.

Transformation takes place in our minds. We must start with our minds, for that is the seat of the soulish realm.

When our spirit is born again, our spirit has to take a position in control over the body and the soul. Even as a man assumes authority and responsibility for the household of which he is a part, over which he guides, directs and protects his family, so such is the very will of God.

What is God's perfect will?

God's perfect will is God's Word. God's Word is His Will. If you want to know God's will, you must study His Word, and His Word is His perfect will. God is perfect and He has a perfect will, and you are either in His will, or you are out of His will.

Some may say, "Why didn't God stop me, if it wasn't His will?" It is because God loves His children, and He gives choice, or the right to choose what a person shall do. And because many refuse to do what God asks them to do, they become rebellious persons.

16

First Samuel 15:23 reads:

> **For rebellion is as the sin of witchcraft, and stubbornness is as iniquity and idolatry....**

We as Christians must understand that when the Spirit of God begins to speak to us, we need to obey that Spirit and do what God asks us to do. And as we follow the leading of the Holy Spirit we will never go astray. *The will of God will never lead you where the grace of God cannot keep you.*

5
Be Renewed by the Word of God

The way to be sure that you are in the perfect will of God is to be renewed in the Spirit *of your mind.*

The question that needs to be asked is this: do you really need to renew your mind?

Perhaps you have experienced God in your spirit and in your soul and in many other areas, such as the healing of your body. But for all that, does your mind need to be renewed in the Word of God? That is a question you must answer between yourself and God.

You just cannot say, "Well, I don't think so." You have to answer the question whether or not your mind needs to be renewed.

You must use this as an example. When the people were delivered out of Egypt, their minds were not renewed by God's Word except Caleb and Joshua. It was God's perfect will for them to be delivered out of Egypt and to go to Canaan land, which God had prepared for them.

Was it God's will that they die in the desert?

Of course not! God didn't choose the desert life for them. God told them to go to Canaan and find the land that was flowing with milk and honey. But because of the human element based on reasoning and the overwhelming fear of giants that they saw there, the Israelites walked around the mountain for 40 years except of course, Caleb and Joshua, who had said, *My God is bigger than the giants in Canaan.*

Many persons are living in doubt and are afraid to trust in God's Word completely in healing or in the "speaking in tongues" because their minds are not illuminated and renewed with God's Word. Paul says in 2 Timothy 1:7:

For God hath not given us the spirit of fear; but of power, and of love, and of a sound *mind*.

Too often, people say, "Why do I need to speak in tongues, and what will happen to me when I speak in tongues?"

I'll tell you what's going to happen to you. You are going to communicate with God the Father, through Jesus Christ, and love the brethren and Jesus more! You are not going to be a better Baptist; you're not going to be a better Methodist; you are not going to be a better Catholic; but you are going to be a better *Christian* than you've ever been before, because you are going to be closer to Jesus.

You are not going to worship a denomination *per se*, but you will, in your mind, speak to God as He requires you to do (John 4:23-24). You are going to worship Jesus. Even in your denominational church, bless God!

There is nothing wrong with denominational churches. I praise God for them. But when they make the denomination their god and are afraid to move out for God, then they have surrendered their minds and their wills to a force other than God.

That's what happened to the Israelites in the desert; they were afraid to move out and go to the promised land.

God's will is for you to know Jesus more and more and to have power in your life.

The people in different denominations have seen the salvation of God. I thank God for that! I'm not knocking denominations. Please do not misunderstand me. I'm using them as an example, so you can see how these things do happen.

Now, these men came with a report which they had observed with their natural eyes and said: "Oh, there are big giants in Canaan land. We better not try to go there." And some people (in the denominations) have told you, "Oh! It is not for today. You better not even try it." But God's Word says...it *is* for today! So who are you going to believe? Especially when the Word says that **God is not a man that he should lie** (Num. 23:19).

Can you imagine walking around the same mountain for 40 years? Do you believe that God had chosen for them to die there in the desert? Of course not, the people themselves chose to do what they did. So do not blame God for your unbelief and fears. Blame the devil, for he is responsible for it.

God is perfect, and God has a perfect will for you and me.

Some have asked me, ''Well, Brother Bill, do you believe that a person can be healed if he does not speak in heavenly tongues?''

Yes, he can.

Then you say, ''Well, can I lay hands on someone else and that someone else will be healed?''

Surely you can. Because God's Word says, the *believer* shall lay hands on the sick and the sick shall recover (Mark 16:18). The Bible says, be it unto you according to your faith (Matt. 9:29). Salvation is for the sinner, but when you become a Christian, the infilling of the Holy Spirit is for you — that you may have power over the devil and be a powerful witness for Christ.

Why should any Christian doubt the Word of God?

I'll tell you why. For the god of this world hath blinded their minds, and they cannot understand the things of God for. . .**they are spiritually discerned** (1 Cor. 2:5-14).

Now these men in the desert saw miracles. And I am sure that you have experienced miracles in your church. I am sure that you have seen people born again. I am sure you have seen people being healed. I am sure that you have seen the joy of the Lord come upon them. I am sure that you've seen people being touched by the power of God. I'm sure that you've seen these things happen in your own church, and praise God for that.

But these men in the desert also saw miracles. However, they never got to the perfect promise of God, which was Canaan land. They saw God give them water out of a rock. They saw God give them food from heaven. Their shoes never wore out on their feet and "there was not one feeble person among their tribes," after they were delivered out of Egypt and obeyed God's Word.

Psalm 107:20 says,

> **He sent his word, and healed them, and delivered them from their destructions.**

Now, if that is true, then what about you and me, as Christians, who are bought with the blood of Jesus, who is the one Mediator of a better covenant, which was established upon better promises? (Hebrews 8:6.)

There are people who say, "I'm afraid, I don't understand."

None of us really understand everything about God, but by *faith* we receive Him and we *trust* Him, because He delivered us out of the hand of our enemies that we might serve Him without fear.

John 14:15 says,

> **If you love me, then keep my commandments.**

Now, what are the commandments of God? In Mark 12:30 He is saying:

> **And thou shalt love the Lord thy God with all thy heart, and with all thy soul, and with all thy mind, and with all thy strength: this is the first commandment.**

That means you are going to have to take authority and you are going to have to say this, "Mind, I am going to accept the Word of God, everything that He says in the Bible, I'm going to accept and believe. It's mine, because God said so! I believe it, and I receive it. No matter what other people may say, I believe the Word of God by *faith* and not by sight" (2 Corinthians 5:7).

If you obey God's commandment, then you are going to love the brethren. Because in Mark 12:31 we read,

> **And the second** (commandment) **is like, namely this, Thou shalt love thy neighbor as thyself....**

When someone comes to you and says, ''Well, it's not of God, it's of the devil.'' And whatever else they think about you, you are going to love them in spite of what they say.

> ...because greater is he that is in you, that he that is in the world.
>
> 1 John 4:4

If you truly love God, you are going to obey His commandments, and you will realize that it is not how great your love is for them, but how great His love is in you.

Remember: God did not send His Word to great men; He sent His Word to make men great.

6
The True Worshiper

Please note in John 4:23 that God the Father is looking and searching for true worshipers and believers, here on earth. Jesus says:

But the hour cometh, and now is, when the *true worshippers* shall worship the Father in spirit and in truth for the Father seeketh such to worship him.

According to Jesus' statement, there is a true worshiper, and a true believer.

Now let's ask ourselves a question, "Who is a true worshiper?" According to what Jesus says in John 4:24,

God is a Spirit: and they that worship him *must worship him in spirit* and in truth.

A true worshiper is the one who worships the Father in Spirit and in truth.

You might have another question such as:"How can I worship God in Spirit and truth?" Speaking in the heavenly language in the Spirit to the Father through Jesus (the Truth). This is what the Bible teaches us — who the true worshiper is — and how to pray a perfect prayer.

You will have to make up your mind that you are going to obey the Word of God, no matter how foolish it might sound to your mind. Tell your doubts and fears to depart from you in Jesus' name, and in place of it ask Jesus to fill you with His Holy Spirit and power; receive your heavenly language and by faith open your mouth and start speaking to Him in your new language (Acts 2:4).

Who is the true believer? The Bible says any person who confesses that Jesus Christ is the Son of God, accepts Him as the Lord of his life and believes in his heart that God raised Him from the dead is a believer.

And these signs shall follow them that believe; In my name shall they cast out devils (evil spirits)**; they shall speak with new tongues;**

. . . they shall lay hands on the sick, and they shall recover.

Mark 16:17,18

However, I wish to emphasize very strongly, that speaking in the heavenly language is not the goal, but a means to reach the goal. The goal of every Christian is the fellowship of love in Christ Jesus (1 Cor. 1:9). We can have many gifts operating in our lives, but if we don't have love we are nothing and we are become as sounding brass or as a tinkling cymbal, and it soon disappears, but love never fails (1 Cor. 13:1-8).

As we read in John 14:6,

Jesus saith unto him, I am the way, the *truth* and the life: no man cometh unto the Father, but by me.

I want you to note the word *truth*. Here Jesus is saying that He is the truth. And John 4:24 told us to "worship the Father in spirit and in truth." You pray in the Spirit (in tongues), and you go through Jesus who is the Truth, to God the Father. And the answer comes from God the Father, through Jesus and the Holy Spirit, to your spirit that dwells in you. That is how you pray a perfect prayer. That's how you know your relationship with God the Father through the spirit.

All of this happens firstly in your mind. You will have to surrender your mind, and say to God, "I bring my mind; I bring my intellect; I bring all my emotions, and I give them to you, Jesus! And I ask you, Lord Jesus, that your blood cleanse my emotions, my feelings, my mind and my will."

That doesn't mean that you are going to lose your will. It means that your will is now on the side of God. Your will will be like His will, and His will will be like your will, and now the mind is being renewed, and your spirit and God's Spirit will become one (1 Cor. 6:17).

Now let me say this...in Ephesians 4:23,24 the Bible says,

> **And be renewed in the spirit of your mind:**
>
> **And that ye put on the new man, which after God is created in righteousness and true holiness.**

When we do this, then our minds become like His mind. Philippians 2:5 reads,

> **Let this mind be in you, which was also in Christ Jesus.**

You see, when you put on the new man, then your mind will be the mind of Christ Jesus.

7

Look Beyond the Mountain

When Jesus said that He was doing the works of the Father, He said,

> **If I do not the works of my Father, believe me not.**

> **But if I do, though ye believe not me, believe the works: that ye may know, and believe, that the Father is in me, and I in Him.**
> **John 10:37,38**

You see, Jesus wasn't *doing His own thing*. He was doing the *Father's will*. For He said in the Garden of Gethsemane, **...not my will, but thine be done** (Luke 22:42).

Why did Jesus surrender His will to the Father?

Because He had complete faith and trust in God the Father!

If we want to be like Jesus, we have to do what Jesus did and surrender our will to the Father. I can assure you that Jesus did not want to die on the cross, because the Bible says that He cried out,

> **O my Father, if it be possible, let this cup pass from me: nevertheless not as I will, but as thou wilt.**
> **Matthew 26:39**

He surrendered His will to the Father, and He went to the cross.

When Jesus went to the cross, He was not looking to see the suffering of the cross. He was looking to the victory thereafter. As He looked at the victory, He was willing to go, and that's when He said, ''Father, not my will, but thy will be done.''

We read in Hebrews 12:2,

> **Looking unto Jesus, the author and finisher of our faith;** *who for the joy that was set before him endured the cross,* **despising the shame, and is set down at the right hand of the throne of God.**

What was the joy?

He was rejoicing because He now saw Himself in the spirit seated at the right hand of the Father as He was looking beyond the cross. The cross before Him was a reality but Jesus was not looking at the reality but at the finality.

You too may have a cross to bear. You too may have a mountain like Jesus had. But if *you'll look beyond the mountain,* and *look to the victory* on the opposite side of the mountain, you will endure it with joy.

Jesus said that He *endured the cross with joy.* He wasn't looking at the suffering, He was *looking at the victory.*

So often we, in our minds, when we get to the cross we say, "Oh, I don't want to die, I don't want to die!" And we stay there. What we need to do is to make up our minds that we aren't going to stop at the cross, we're going on. Praise God!

In Colossians 3:10, Paul speaks about the mind.

> **And have put on the new man, which is renewed in knowledge after the image of him that created him.**

Where is knowledge stored? Knowledge is stored in your mind. Everything that you learn is stored right there in your "computer" which is your mind. You must renew your mind daily with His Word to *change* your thinking, to think like Jesus, and be renewed in Him who created you.

And then he says, **Walk in the Spirit** (Gal. 5:16). When you renew your mind, you're going to walk in the spirit. When you walk in the spirit, you will not fulfill the works of the flesh.

What are the works of the flesh?

> Now the works of the flesh are manifest, which
> are these; Adultery, fornication, uncleanness,
> lasciviousness,
>
> Idolatry, witchcraft, hatred, variance, emulations,
> wrath, strife, seditions, heresies,
>
> Envyings, murders, drunkenness revellings....
>
> Galatians 5:19-21

When you walk in the spirit you will not let the works of the flesh defile you.

What is meant by walking in the spirit? How do you put on a spirit? Well, if I asked you to put on a dress or a suit, that means you are going to be clothed with it. It has to cover you. If you are going to swim, you have to get into the water and let it cover you.

When you walk in the spirit, it means you are going to clothe your mind with the Word of God, and let it swim in His Word, allowing your born again spirit, by the Holy Spirit, to take control of your body and soul.

How are you going to get into the spirit?

By renewing your mind and walking in love.

To walk in love means to walk in Jesus, to think and talk like Jesus. Philippians 4:8 tells us,

> ...whatsoever things are true, whatsoever things
> are honest, whatsoever things are just, whatsoever
> things are pure, whatsoever things are lovely,
> whatsoever things are of a good report; if there be any
> virtue, and if there be any praise, think on these
> things.

He says *think* about these things.

That's something that we need to learn as Christians. If we can't find something good to talk about, or think about, and if we can't walk in love, then we need to *renew our minds with the Word*. The Word will bring us into a *positive* response, a *positive* thought.

The Bible says be very quick to see and to hear, but be very slow to speak. This is something all of us need to learn.

8
Spiritual Weapons

In Galatians 2:20 Paul said,

I am crucified with Christ: nevertheless I live; yet not I, but Christ liveth in me: and the life which I now live in the flesh I live by the faith of the Son of God, who loved me, and gave himself for me.

You can see it now...Paul was walking in love. Jesus is *love*.

He that loveth not knoweth not God; for God is love.

1 John 4:8

If we walk in Jesus, we walk in love. If we walk in love, we walk in Jesus. That's why Paul could say that, because he walked in the love of Jesus. People condemned him, hurt him and hated him, but Paul still loved them, because he realized that he was in a spiritual battle.

You cannot fight a spiritual battle of sin with carnal weapons. You are going to have to realize, like Jehoshaphat realized when he looked at the armies that were coming against him in 2 Chronicles 20 and he said, "I don't have any weapons." God said, "You don't need any weapons, because you have Jehovah, the God Almighty Himself, who will come and fight the battle for you." God said, "It's not your battle, it's my battle, but the victory is yours."

What you need to recognize is that the battle over the devil has been won by Jesus Christ, who gave us spiritual weapons and commanded us to occupy until He comes. Christ requires of us to trust in His Word and have the obedience of a Jehoshaphat.

For the weapons of our warfare are not carnal, but mighty through God to the pulling down of strong-holds;

Casting down imaginations, and every high thing that exalteth itself against the knowledge of God, and bring into captivity every thought to the *obedience of Christ Jesus*.

I will give you an illustration on what I'm talking about...

While teaching at Oral Roberts University, I ran an experiment with a group of my students who were studying the Russian language. (Many persons had said to me that the Russian language was difficult, and how could they learn it, and I would say to them that they were defeated in their minds by their negative confession.) I assigned to my students these songs to be memorized in Russian, *Power in the Blood, How Great Thou Art* and *Redeemed*. I also assigned to them several secular songs. They got their secular songs memorized in a matter of two or three days, and were doing a great job of singing them. I gave them another song, *Kalinka*. It had real rhythm, and they were really charged up.

They would come to class and rejoice as we sang *Kalinka*. We sang for the first five or ten minutes, and then I said, "I want you to memorize *How Great Thou Art*.

Six weeks before finals I assigned those songs, and one girl who was an "A" student wanted to quit one week before finals and taken an "F" in the course because the devil had convinced her that she could not do it. She came into my office and said, "I can't do it."

The next day I took them out of class and said, "Leave your books here and we're going to the brook." It was a beautiful day. We went to the brook and sat under a shade tree. I had told them the day before to bring their Bibles, that we were going to study our Bibles, too.

I showed them in the Word of God that they were in a spiritual battle.

> **For though we walk in the flesh, we do not war after the flesh.**
>
> **2 Corinthians 10:3**

You can't fight this enemy with weapons, like guns, bombs or bows and arrows. This enemy, the devil, is a *spirit*.

How are you going to fight the devil?

You will have to use spiritual weapons to fight this spiritual enemy.

When we sat down, I told them that they had worked hard with their minds, but the devil was keeping them from learning. He had a place in their minds and was telling them, "No, you can't remember. You cannot pronounce those words."

The devil was doing everything he could to keep them from studying. Many of them were willing to take an "F" if they did not have to memorize the songs.

I said, "You must memorize the songs. This is going to be your final examination. If you don't take the final, then you can't pass the course."

I tell you, when they saw the Scriptures and realized how powerful and great the verses were, the students actually ran home from that place to study and memorize their songs.

The next morning, a student was at my office at 7:00 a.m. and he had learned the three songs overnight! He took authority over that demon that kept him from receiving the Word of God into his spirit. He took authority over his mind, and he sat there and learned it.

He said, "It took me a little time, but I've got the victory!"

Bless God, he learned the three songs that I asked them to memorize — overnight!

When the finals come, every student received an "A", because every student knew the songs.

I am telling you this because I want to show you that there is a spiritual *battle in the mind,* and you will have to renew your mind, if you desire to win your spiritual battles and confess that you are what the Word says you are, and your confession will become your possession. **For as he thinketh in his heart, so is he...** (Prov. 23:7).

You must understand that God is *stronger than the devil.* You don't have to take a back seat because God has given you the front seat.

You must confess (say it with your mouth), and what you confess you will possess;

> For verily I say unto you, That whosoever shall say unto this mountain, Be thou removed, and be thou cast into the sea; and shall not doubt in his heart, but shall believe that those things which he saith shall come to pass; he shall have whatsoever he saith.
>
> Therefore I say unto you, What things soever ye desire, when ye pray, believe that ye receive them, and ye shall have them.
>
> Mark 11:23,24

If you are going to believe John 3:16, then bless God, believe on God's blessings as well. He wants you to have the blessings of health. He wants you to have the victory over the devil in your spirit, soul and body.

If you want victory, then you are going to have to believe and appropriate 2 Corinthians 10:3-5:

> For though we walk in the flesh, we do not war after the flesh:
>
> (For the weapons of our warfare are not carnal, but mighty through God to the pulling down of strongholds;)
>
> *Casting down imaginations,* and every high thing that exalteth itself against the knowledge of God, and *bringing into captivity every thought to the obedience of Christ.*

You are a sum total of your spiritual Father, and your heart will confess it.

> O generation of vipers, how can ye, being evil, speak good things? for out of the abundance of the heart the mouth speaketh.
>
> Matthew 12:34